Abba God, The Master Poet

Raven Chasity Rogers

ISBN Number: 979-8-9908073-2-7
LCC Number: 2025906641

Abba God, The Master Poet
Copyright © 2025 Raven Chasity Rogers
Edited by Cynthia M. Portalatín
Published by Maynetre Manuscripts, LLC
PO Box 1819, Owings Mills, MD 21117
www.maynetre.com

This is a work of fiction. Names, characters, places, and incidents are products of the author's imagination, the author's own personal experience, or are used fictitiously and are not to be construed as real. While the author was inspired in part by actual events, the characters are not distantly inspired by any individual known or unknown to the author. Any resemblance to actual events, locales, business establishments, organizations, or persons, living or dead, is entirely coincidental.

Printed in the United States of America
First Printing 2025
10 9 8 7 6 5 4 3 2 1

Contents

Book 4: Abba God, The Master Poet

Dedication

This fourth book is dedicated to God, the Father. Every good gift and every perfect gift is from above, and cometh down from the Father of lights, with whom is no variableness, neither shadow of turning. (James 1:17 KJV)

Psalm 24:7:10 (KJV)

7 Lift up your heads, O ye gates; and be ye lift up, ye everlasting doors; and the King of glory shall come in.

8 Who is this King of glory? The Lord strong and mighty, the Lord mighty in battle.

9 Lift up your heads, O ye gates; even lift them up, ye everlasting doors; and the King of glory shall come in.

10 Who is this King of glory? The Lord of hosts, he is the King of glory. Selah.

Book 1: God Sent The Raven

The Author of My Soul
12/12/2022

Many, many years ago,
Lord, You wrote the storyline for my life.
The script written wasn't anything strange to you.
Because You drafted me to be blessed and determined to pass
right through.
This life is not fiction!
It is surely a fact!
The way You modify me, when I fall.
Immediately, You bless me to bounce right back.
God, You possess the script to my soul!
Only the narration of Your words can instantly make me
whole!
The pleasure of having You as the author, grants me a life
worth living!
And the purpose to fulfill Your will is the ultimate gift You
are giving!

The Essence of You
11/20/2022

The essence of You Lord …
Takes my breath away
Enlightens me to say
Strengthens me from day-to-day
Is where I lay

The essence of You, Lord …
Is what so many can't find
Gives me peace of mind
Displays a love so gentle and kind
Is there all the time

The essence of You, Lord …
Grants me direction, wherever I go
Is who, and what I know
So magnificent, You always show
Plays a harmonious flow

Abba God, The Master Poet

The essence of You, Lord
Leaves me impressed
Is always the best
Is worth fulfilling this beautiful quest
Provides to my unique soul rest

The Ultimate Homie
11/27/2022

I get to share You with the world.
No magnifying glass, full exposure!
There's no need for an acquaintance, the dopest Best Friend!
Yes! I'm sure!
I pray and submit the most deepest of secrets, before walking out the front door.
You handle all of my business, and it builds trust, more and more!
I opened my heart to help enemies, who stared me down to the floor.
And like the Ultimate Homie, Your power allowed me to soar.
In clear visions and dreams, You reveal to me, who you are!
The Magnificent Holy Spirit!
The real star that You are!
Some may never understand Your presence and deny the power there of.
But just like Jesus, the Heavenly Son, You also came from above.

Abba God, The Master Poet

Hallelujah! All the glory!
The best of friendships, you see!
Thank You, Ultimate Homie for always guiding me!

A Mirror of Me
11/28/2022

Open your eyes! Look up! What do you see?
Is it a reflection of Jesus all over me?
A mirror image of His character, from His word, to speak
life!
If you see Him, right through me, no need to think twice.
To walk, talk and follow after true righteousness!
That beautiful mirror of me, you can see at its best!

The Power of My Tears
11/24/2022

The power of my tears
So gentle flowing from my eyes
Developed from the pain of rejection and abandonment
Formed deeply inside
False accusations with no explanation
They continue to stream down my face
The extreme challenges that life had to offer
Left me feeling distant and too out of place
A waterfall of anger, I had to leave it ALL behind
But the power of my tears washed it away!
Bringing love, joy, and new life to mind!

A Bittersweet Lullaby
11/27/2022

Cradle me to sleep with your love, as your words of affirma-
tion, serenade my ears, like a bittersweet lullaby.
As I hear the beating of your heart, it gives off lovely music
notes, with a pitch so high.
Sing to me with the sound of your breath!
Inhale and exhale, to the harmony of you rocking me back
and forth in your arms.
The peaceful melody of your love, is an escape from all the
chaos and harm.
Flawlessly written and to my surprise,
When I embrace the act of your goodness and bittersweet
lullaby!

Crimson Love
11/15/2022

Your love is red and sharp
I wear it like the latest fashion
Leaves me so mesmerized!
Sometimes, I don't know what happened

Like bright elements of a solar eclipse
Just can't stare with my eyes
The crimson color so deep
It's the sweetest surprise!

Overflows, like a manifold of blessings,
It makes me want to scream
Feels like an evangelical sensation
If you know what I mean.

Rose Petals
11/28/2022

Silky! Soft and elegant!
With a touch of your grace.
The softness of your character, adds a special touch to my
face.
Separated, but when joined together, depicts a symbol of our
love.
It's the combination of your greatness!
Designed from Heaven above.

That Great Commencement!
11/27/2022

Congratulations, Graduates!
The day has finally come
Where your hard work has paid a ton.
A ton of time, sacrifice and tears, because you didn't quit!
You now stand here!
Standing tall, head held high!
Let the loud sound of Victory, reach the sky!
The sky above is where you'll soar.
For some, the first of generations, an absolute score!
A score for the ages, as you carry on with success.
Walk in the path, where the light shines and walk into your best!
So many have come from near and far, For higher education; you set the bar.
A bar so heavy, it takes a special grace to carry.
To carry the load with patience, was enough to tarry.
Your best is what's appreciated! No matter what they say!
Remember this moving forward, every start of the day is a new day!
A new day to conquer all that's set before you,

Raven Chasity Rogers

As you climb over rocky challenges, like the shining morning Sun.
Recite this over your spirit! Indeed, I have already Won!
Won the reward, because someone greater paved the way before me. And now that time has come!
To celebrate that Great Commencement!
Congratulations, Graduates, all the hard work is done!!!

God Sent the Raven!!!
11/28/2022

Good day all, my name is Raven.
Born and raised in Jersey City.
Please don't feel sorry for me! Don't need none of your pity.
God sent the Raven
Marked by the Most High, since the beginning of
time!
Some great days more than others, I put that on a dime!
Hated by some, but always loved by so many.
A family fortune! Can't complain!
I have plenty!
Misunderstood, while I walked out this walk.
The prime focus to many, but the least one to talk!
God sent the Raven to the Earth, to bring Glory to His name!
So, please get out of my way, if you're not doing the same!

Reflection

Who do you think each poem within the section "God Sent The Raven" is written to?

What comes to mind as you read each poem in this section?

What's your favorite line (s) in each poem within this section?

If you had to add another stanza to each poem within this section, what would you write?

Other Thoughts

Book 2: Jesus (Holy Spirit) Is My Ghostwriter

You Are the King of My Heart!
1/11/2023

Being summoned before Your face, I come humbly
before you.
Extraordinary, You are! With no one else to submit to.
Your honor and dignity are what my heart is yielding
towards.
Willingly, I submit all that I am, while releasing every cord.
Each and every part of my heart, Your Highness, I lay it
gently at your feet.
Invited by the presence of Your power, what a great way to
meet!
Empty, I come before the mercy of Your throne.
Symbolizing that sacred place!
Getting pass the nervousness that I'm feeling all over me.
Remaining calm with ease, doing whatever it takes.
No judgment necessary coming from the grace of Your
throne.
Your spoken word, spoken over my heart, is a sincere word
alone.
With love, You accept even the flawed parts of me, being the
King of my heart.

Restoring and releasing me on my way, granting me a refreshing new start!

Oh My, GREATNESS!
3/18/2023

Oh my, Greatness!
God, You are at it again.
Allowing me to pen another outstanding poem.
May I begin?

You compose the softness of your word.
Falling fresh upon me, like A Pleasant Reign.
With much to appreciate, Your greatness is evident. As they
Sit Back and Watch Me grow.
I can't complain!

Oh my, Greatness, You demolish the darkness by declaring,
O' Son-shine for me today!
In all radiance, and a reminder To My Future, I walk in
victory! There's no delay!

To commune, and attached with laughter, we developed A
Friendship So Deep.
In Your hand, I present An Invitation So Tender. My heart is
yours to keep!

Thank you again as You Safeguard Me with your unfailing
presence.
And Just In Case they need to know,
It is to You, I give reverence!

A Poem of Salvation
3/27/2023

Today is the right day to be set free.
Confess with your mouth and believe
in your heart, the Lord Jesus,
so that your soul may live with Him in eternity.
He is waiting to receive you! Love,
with open arms.
Be not afraid! Come forward, my child, there
is no need to be alarmed.
The price for your sins has already
been paid on Calvary.
Hallelujah! Thank you, Jesus!
For giving us the VICTORY!!!

BLESSED Sexy!
2/05/2023

Anointed, compassionate and special in your sight.
I am amazing, strong and given the power to fight.
Here's a new term that will surely make your day.
The words are BLESSED SEXY and are here to stay!
That's right! Yeah, I said it! Here it is! Yup, it's true!
Shower down from the high throne to shape its form in
the new.
BLESSED SEXY to be chosen from my mother's womb.
BLESSED SEXY from the one who created the stars, sun and
moon.
BLESSED SEXY when I walk in His grace with liberty.
BLESSED SEXY because His dear Son died for you and died
for me.
BLESSED SEXY being grateful, while receiving His very
best!
BLESSED SEXY stepping into that Holy glow, nothing else
to say. You get the rest!

On Blessed Knee
3/20/2023

You awaken me with a thirst and a yearning
to see what today will be.
Coming humbly before You, with singing on my lips, while
down on blessed knee.
Surrendering all my struggles and happiness before Your
remarkable throne.
I'm reminded by You, throughout the day, that I am
NEVER alone.
A complete zeal for the purpose set before me, to live out
each and every day.
On blessed knee, awaiting instruction.
Nevertheless, to You I pray.
Without Your word, I don't have the light afforded for me
to see.
That's why daily I must take the time to seek
You, kneeling down on blessed knee.

A Scarlet Harvest
3/18/2023

His blood protects my harvest from the fountain tongue of
your weak language.
A solace, being covered by the power of His scarlet blood, is
a gift and a privilege.
Shattering every weapon at your disposal,
you're already facing defeat!
I do not wrestle against flesh and blood, 'cause
I relinquish all of my cares at his feet.
The crops and my harvest, are not affected by your
weakness and your vain glory.
After all, I overcome by the blood of the Lamb, and
the words of my blessed true story!

Black Pearl of Radiance
3/25/2023

Perfected and shielded with a flawless melanin coating, quite astonishing, I'm sure!
The UV rays of sunshine given enhance one to explore.
Handcrafted in different colors, shades and sizes – embodied to be loved.
The authenticity of the black pearl, an insightful piece and one of a kind, cannot be shoved.
In its rarest form, too diligent, an imitator cannot compare.
The beauty of a black pearl so radiant, one will say; so envious, it really is not fair!
A sparkling result, brightly shining from a distance, yet hidden away for a specific time.
I am so thankful to be one of them, a justly fortune, rightfully mine!
From the ancestors of past generations, equipped and strong women glazed by the glow.
The footprints of their triumphant victories have been planted upon all of us to grow.
Ladies, black pearls of radiance, with open arms embrace that you are different! This is you!

And don't ever embellish the birth right that is yours for the taking. Genuinely, this you do!

Lavender Love
3/18/2023

Can't you tell at this point, that I'm a blessed romantic?
Obviously, if you saw what I've been through, you'll know
why, it's not magic!
Colors seem to bring out the best love and joy all around us.
Let me acknowledge the fact: the visual effects of it are a
bonus!
Lavender is a beautiful color! What's not there about it to
love?
It sparks a joy on the inside, that can only come from Heaven
above.
A display of grace and serenity, that's how I desire my love
life to be.
To walk with a calm sense of elegance. The way God intends
for it to be.
The dynamics of this color are worth every dividend and all
royalties.
Lavender love hold close to me, defining all of the remark-
able abilities!

Yellow Spring
3/24/2023

Sunflowers, yellow Lillie's and sunshine galore.
It is Springtime! Everyone, listen up! There are fun times in store.
Eating hotdogs from the hotdog stand, adding mustard on them, you know what's up
Lemonade refreshing and cold to drink, let me have a large one and fill the cup!
A yellow blimp flying high, kissing up to the clear blue sky.
Watching the dog chase after the yellow frisbee, as I am gladly walking by.
Yellow canaries singing sweet music leaving a gentle fragrance in the air.
I am overjoyed with so much cheer! Springtime, it's my favorite season of the year.

Jesus (Holy Spirit) Is My Ghostwriter
3/3/2023

A pleasant and lovely day readers, whoever you are!
He's so powerful! No introduction needed thus far!
It is plain to see, He's where my help cometh from.
The original ghostwriter, penning these stanzas from
day one.
The rules of His writings are an epic game changer.
He blessed the words of each line, to shine brighter. Look
out! DANGER!

Allow me to explain! God Sent the Raven.
The whole time it was Him, giving great words to pen.
There's not a doubt in my mind, just like The Ultimate
Homie, He will always defend!
I couldn't come up with powerful words like this, on the best
of my days.
Please let me have the honor to state: it's whatever He says!

He was the Author To My Soul, the whole time; give Him
credit!

Raven Chasity Rogers

As I Stargaze upon His marvelous splendor, always! You
should have read it!
Every single word written by Him. Many Ventures, that's
how I am living and how I got through.
It's okay if you choose to walk in unbelief. Step aside! In
faith, I'm believing for you!

Because There's A Story Behind Those Eyes, to tell the truth
no retreating!
Dear Blue Skies, will you come out today and give us that
beautiful greeting?
Much to prepare, and so much on my mind.
The experience of writer's block, Lord please help! The
words I can't find!

You spoke to me saying, Forget Fear! I am with you this day!
To address that Great Commencement, no matter what
comes my way.
And like the Invisible Butterfly, it is a challenge to see.
Oh, so speedily, You came up with this masterpiece written
for me.

Lord, My Daddy, My Heart, You speak a message to
everyone as they flip through the pages.
No discrimination is welcome! Your words of wisdom, a
guarantee for all ages.
Now, that the truth is out there and my cover is blown,
I don't care if Home Rejected Me, because Your greatest love
sits high on the throne.

Reflection

Who do you think each poem within the section "Jesus (Holy Spirit) Is My Ghostwriter" is written to?

What comes to mind as you read each poem in this section?

What's your favorite line (s) in each poem within this section?

If you had to add another stanza to each poem within this section, what would you write?

Other Thoughts

Book 3: Lord, You Supply The Main Ingredients

God, the Honorable!
5/27/2023

Again, I say, Greater is the One who dwells on the inside of
me, than the irrelevant one in the world.
I present to You out of a cheerful heart, because
I am that grateful girl!
You enable your Son to cause my light to shine, and
ALL of the credit goes to You!
Because the breath of life, feels good throughout, sending
praises up to Heaven, is what I do!
Cover my visions and dreams from the corruptive naysayers,
trying to creep in unaware; so they tarry.
Chaperone over the harvest that is waiting for me to gather
graciously, without me being weary!
God, You are worth every mention! It is impossible to
complete with anyone else, and that's why I come to know,
Your love for me shows clearly!

Yes, God Did It Right!!!
5/15/2023

Stampede over all seen and unseen warfare, please,
throughout the night!
Sanitize my mind fully in Your word, to overcome this fight!
Sacred are Your ways to help me live right!
Surround me around loving people; now, that is real tight!
Set my eyes upon You daily; grant me with spiritual insight!
Surely, Your paths are made clear, 'cause You are my light!
Sever the hand of the enemy, with Your power and Your
might!
Submitting to Your will! Allow my life to take flight!
Sowing seeds of His goodness within me, for a
harvest delight!
Surrender all my cares directly to You, so I don't need to be
uptight!
Spotting my inconsistencies, forgive me, Lord! There's a new
spark to ignite!
Searching my heart leaving no room, for evil words to recite!
Subtitles to the words of Your songs, singing praises forever!
It's alright!

Abba God, The Master Poet

Shouting loud in triumphant victories, more and more, make room for love; lets unite!

You Are My Real Promise
4/7/2023

Since then, I wondered, why? How could You speak such a prophetic melody over me, when I didn't walk in Your way?
In fact, it was Your love that looked beyond my fault, quite noticeable on that wooden cross for display!
You protect me from the false narratives, of the doubters, whose actions hold no type of weight.
Every outcome works out beautifully, no matter what the state!
A realm of remarkability, show me as my heart is curious to explore!
Because my soul yearns for Your effervescent purpose, to saturate me more and more!
Absorbing from that moment, a major covenant keeper. You're the real blessing! I receive!
Your every word spoken over my destiny, an orchestrated harmony, I believe!
A dissertation proven factually, no one can take away Your truth planted in me.
As long as I stand firm on Your solid foundation, my special rock, You remain to be!

Beautified F.A.I.T.H.
5/20/2021

FOREVER and ever, I will believe, even when the blessing is not yet tangible!
AWARDED by God, the Perfect One, because I realize and trust, that He is surely able!
IN agreement with His purpose for my life, despite the vicissitudes, He will dismantle!
THE Only Supernatural being throughout the universe, who illuminates my life to shine bright!
HIGHEST in regards giving all Honor due; accepting everything about Him is extremely right!

I Am the Beautiful
6/1/2023

It becomes a mandate for me, during this time, to appreciate
life more and not settle for less!
I am the beautiful elegance flowing through the fabric of a
captivating and whimsical dress!
I am the beautiful presence changing atmospheres in the
room, because I am not here for the mess!
I am the beautiful painting on the canvas, a special piece, a
true work of art!
I am the beautiful writer sharing my gift with an audience, as
I reveal what's on my heart!
I am the beautiful creation secretly hidden, not yet discov-
ered, but one of a kind!
I am the beautiful flower blooming in its season, a great
asset, yet rare to find!
I am the beautiful radiance to brighten up your day, giving
you the strength to keep going!
I am the beautiful spirit filled with a purpose, looking up to
the Highest, to keep on flowing!

Chocolate Covered Miracles
4/10/2023

The impact will set off alarms, an explosive banger of
expansion!
Holy Spirit opening Supernatural doors, catapulting me to
another dimension!
Visual effects seen of His gentleness and mercies to help
everything just settle in.
The beginning of the most breathtaking life story, a new
chapter written. Here's how it will begin!
Tried by the fire, smoking hot! Can't you see that I am the
apple of His eye?
Rebuking the devourer for my sake, demolishing demons! So
long, you had your try!
Who would have imagined, a gentle morsel, birthed from my
mother's precious womb?
Adopted into His kingdom empire, before Jesus was ever laid
up in the tomb.
It is the marvel of His glory and righteousness, a true love
story, that abounds!
Everything I've been waiting for, I search in Him, a miracle
worker, I have found!

On that note, a caption recognized and fit for the Master's use, He covers me all around!

A Smooth-Like-Butter Transition
4/10/2023

I beseech you all, let's incorporate, have a
fun time and get it in!
Spreading Agape love and good tidings so pleasantly,
It will always win!
Our imperfections, stirred to perfection with a touch of
grace, to walk in that marvelous light!
A smooth transition, rich and creamy like butter, simply
great! It is out of sight!
To embrace what the Lord has done for us; when He says,
you're ready! Arise and move!
It's a transition so necessary, with the right ingredients
added for your good! Yet tangible!
Let me just set this reminder here. It was NEVER about us,
from the very beginning.
Because it was His Son, who paid the price! I don't hear you,
now, what are you saying?
His pure blood runs deeply through our veins, all who
believe and receive! We walk by faith, no need to see!
Hold on and trust Him with an understanding that, one day,
we'll reign with Jesus, so Heavenly!

A Sure Overcomer!
4/19/2023

Sit back and watch me soar over your
head, like an eagle!
Patiently waiting to take off and fly high.
Now, watch what God do!
Prospering like never before! So, please
excuse you!
A testament calling on my life, too
gracious and true!
Flowing in the Holy Spirit, speaking
the real truth!
Glorifying the Highest of High! His praise
surpassing the roof!
Adjust your attitude, because all of His real
love is just remarkable!
Shutting the mouths of naysayers, who talk trash,
but they have no clue!
It's okay! You are forgiven! Please take a breath,
before you turn blue!
A for-sure season, don't give up and wait! Your

turn will come to you!
Meditate on His word, both day and night, and
watch Him follow through!
Overall, don't panic! Everything is alright! We win!
He's always there for you!

Untouchable, I Am
4/2/2023

Touched by His Mighty hand, untouchable to man, that
I Am!
Anointed and chosen since birth, raised
to show respect. Yes, sir and yes, ma'am!
He rebukes the devourer for my sake, even though
I made so many mistakes.
Overshadowed by Him, the enemy has to
get His permission to come my way.
Grateful, 'cause the Greater One lives
inside of me from day-to-day.
Really terrific! You enable me to draw close,
and it's in You I abide!
Thank you for a power truly electric! Permitting every
dark force to flee on every side.
Gladly, I am surrounded and shielded by
Your loving grace.
Your hedge of protection, restricts my enemies from
coming anywhere near my face.
Superb are Your ways! Granting me the favor

to succeed!
And an understanding to hear and do everything
to always stay freed!

Lord, You Supply the Main Ingredients

4/5/2023

God, no other ingredient equals the amount of impeccable goodness, coming from You.
The bread of Life, Your unfailing Love, and Holy Spirit are so powerful to equip me through.
In prayer, by faith I enter humbly, seeking Your Holy presence in the secret place.
By Your Spirit, I am delivered with Your special touch, authority, mercy, and grace!
Lord, You supply A Strawberry Kind of Love, to look past my faults and see my needs.
As I enjoy Your marvelous wonders, pouring out Raspberry Blessings as You take the lead.
Emblazon Your light to the paths ahead by shining a Lemon-Filled Son-Rise, guiding me all the way.
Overjoyed with holiness, filled with Your truth and a Slice of Orange Happiness, You are forever here to stay.

Reflection

Who do you think each poem within the section "Lord, You Supply The Main Ingredients" is written to?

What comes to mind as you read each poem in this section?

What's your favorite line (s) in each poem within this section?

If you had to add another stanza to each poem within this section, what would you write?

Other Thoughts

Book 4: Abba God, The Master Poet

Rapid Skies
6/3/2023

What a remarkable morning to bear witness, by
getting an opportunity to look up high.
To see how the skies provide an atmosphere for
the birds and aircraft flying by.
Moving at a fast pace, it seems like the clouds
are in a competitive sprint race.
It is a beautiful opportunity to experience the vibrant
scenery playing out before my face.
Some want to be a part of the fun and have a taste.
Skydivers, hot air balloons, and fowls of the air. I'm enjoying
that bird's eye view!
Participating as an eyewitness, I desire to grab ahold of
something new.
Rapid movement, soaring at a fast speed. Once you look
away, you will miss all of the action.
The motion picture of the fluffy clouds and flocks of birds,
fly together for a coming attraction.
A marvelous scenery speaking at high volume, with melodic
singing of the gentle canary.

Looking up in total awe, its simplicity is a great amazement for me, no need to tarry.
The outcome is proof, that God has created everything in His time so beautifully!!

Oh My, Jesus
4/1/2024

Time and time again, y'all allow
evil to dwell in your hearts.
It is my mercy, grace, peace, and love
that will NEVER fail or fall apart.
The woman caught in adultery, she was
very fearful for her life.
Scribes and Pharisees, you total hypocrites!
How dare you hunger after strife?
Please! Let me make this clear! Y'all
are truly evil, and that's a sin.
Only in Christ Jesus, will His agape love
always empower you to win!
Yes, she has done wrong, but she is my child.
So, just leave her alone.
He that hath committed no sin come boldly, if
you dare, and cast the first stone.
Search no more! Dry your eyes and get up! The word of God
is the living SEED.
Walk by faith, and not by sight, 'cause Jesus Christ
is everything you will ever need.

Get It Gideon!
3/29/2024

Hey, you! Get up now! Stand firm! Do you know who
you are in God? Take flight!
A mighty man of valor, says the angel of the Lord. Pure
Facts, you know that's right!
No need to hide anymore, threshing wheat by the wine press.
His hope fallen to the ground.
Fear not! You have been chosen by God to destroy the false
idols that are lingering around.
300 mighty warriors are all you will need to fight
this epic battle. Hear them loudly roar!!
Doing total damage to every enemy who comes against you.
Plow through them with might and soar!!
You can do it! I will perform some signs intentionally,
Gideon, to give you hope.
Drying up the fleece with the dew upon the ground - a sign,
proven in the scriptures. God is so dope!
Obedience is the key! Therefore, walk in total faith
to experience true victory.
Trust God, lean not to thine own understanding, and
shout loud in liberty.

Boaz and Ruth: (A Dope Love)
1/16/2024

Have you ever noticed, it's called the book of
Ruth for a reason?
The Moabitess left without a husband, because he
died. It is a new season!
She refused to remain in a land where the gods
of her people were not real.
Leaving everything behind to follow Naomi to
freedom. Yes! It's a sweet deal!

Loyalty, she displayed to her mother-in-law,
the sad widow Naomi.
Traveling to Bethlehem to receive the greatest blessing from
the Living God, Almighty.
The journey to a new land, for a stranger, had
to be a challenge.
Stepping out by faith, sacrificing all that she had,
now that was quite savage!
Gleaning in the wheat fields, she had the privilege,
as a widow, and the right.
Boaz, the kinsman redeemer - she totally found

favor in his sight.

Being in the right place at the right time, without a
doubt, truly matters.
Whom God has joined together, let no other
man or woman try to shatter.
Part of a beautiful lineage that has given birth
to the Wonderful Messiah.
Repent! Give your life! Be set apart and filled
with Holy Ghost fire!
The Great! The Mighty God, the Lord of hosts,
true to His name.
One word from Him, and your life will NEVER,
ever be the same.

The Gift of His Grace
8/7/2024

Gently, You lay your hand upon me.
In Your dwelling place, is the place to be.
With my arms, held up high, You set me free.
Lord, the gift of Your grace, is my remedy.

God, it's Your grace that covers me.
Saturate my life! You are all that I see.
There is no peace if I don't live out this life, holy.
Lord, the gift of Your grace, is my remedy.

Thank you, Lord, for the gift of your grace,
a blessing so refreshing, like a soft touch on my face.
Living in a world in need of Your love; You keep me safe.
Surround me always, by the gift of Your grace

Honestly, I did not deserve it, but you saw fit to give me that
and more.
Protect me from all of the evil. Holy Spirit, outpour.
As Your love blesses me to fly high like an eagle and soar.
Surround me, by the gift of Your grace, like never before.

A Poetic Praise!!
10/15/2023

Come on and give Him glory, today on this date!
The word of God is the truth. No need to debate!
Repent and be Baptized before it's too late!
Some things may seem hard, with a lot on your plate!
Hold on to Christ and have faith in the wait!
I can attest it is not over, and it's not too late!
He's a loving God who does everything great!
Who is always on time! Truly, He's NEVER late!
Get over yourself and push open the gate!
Jesus Christ is true love! Put away all of the hate!
Don't be a hater! Let His agape love populate!
March in assurance, He makes everything great!
Start all over anew, with a clean and fresh slate!
Won't have it no other way. Who else can relate?
Marvelous and humble, He's the PERFECT teammate!
Singing and shouting Hallelujah from a rich, blessed state!

God, All and All!
4/26/2017

Even though I'd lost my way, You took me back.
With no condemnation, It was You all along,
who aligned me on the right track.
God, all and all, Your love plays like a sweet song.

Appreciating the good times and the bad,
Your presence, so beautiful and strong.
Ashamed of my mistakes, I felt sad.
God, all and all, You gave me hope all along

So now, I give my life to You as I open my heart.
Lord, please enter, flow freely through,
and grant me a fresh and new start.
The only one to make me whole, with no doubt.
All and all, I pray Your unconditional love will never go away
nor depart.

Joseph The Fruitful
5/3/2024

Joseph, one of a kind and diligent. A man
of integrity. Where do I begin?
Favored by his father Jacob, born from the womb
of Rachel. The best to ever win!
Envied and hated by his brothers, over an
assignment he didn't ask for.
Obedient and God fearing, name meaning, He will
add. Someone, please total the score!
Sold into slavery for 20 pieces of silver.
Was that all he was worth?
A dreamer gifted by the most High. Accurate interpretations
from God, giving birth.
Second in command to Pharaoh in Egypt, for Him, it was the
right place to be.
As part of the promise, his family; God used him to set them
all free!
Manasseh and Ephraim, two sons born from his seed are
living proof!
That what can only come from God is beauty for ashes. Now,
that is the real truth!

Abba God, The Master Poet

His father, who thought he was dead, saw with his own eyes,
his living legacy.
Joseph, the fruitful and given a coat of many colors,
is now a part of Bible history.

So Just Keep Reppin'
8/15/2023

People, now is the time to rise up,
get on the move, and sound the alarm.
No weapon formed against us shall prosper.
God protects us from all of the harm.
Be not deceived! Jesus is real!
There's no need to deflect, be fake, or get
Discouraged, 'cause He is the real deal!
Jesus loves you more than ever. He paid the price,
and that's no cheap thrill!
It is okay! No need to be mean!
Stop with all of the foolishness, just to be seen.
Speak the word of God instead, and keep it clean!
Deliverance is necessary! The enemy's dark ways will always
come to the light!
In the name of Jesus, I plead the blood. Come out, unclean
spirit; you lost the fight!
Be not afraid! In God we trust; all hope is not lost!
Repent! Be set free, in Jesus' name, because He has paid the
Ultimate cost.
Yes, He is the Creator and the real love

to all of mankind.
Jesus, so Perfect! He was never lost. We are the
ones that he had to find.
So, don't dare get it twisted! It is written, we are saved
by His grace.
Humbly, come seeking him while dwelling spiritually
in the secret place.
Jesus died on the cross to save your soul. A triumphant
victory. Graciously, stand firm and be bold!
He sits on the right hand of God, the Father,
reigning in Heaven.
We are His ambassadors, on earth to spread
his word. So, just keep reppin'!
God will never leave you nor forsake you,
and that is a clear fact!
He sent the Comforter, Holy Spirit. Invite him
into your heart, to keep you on track.
There is a supernatural battle going on
in the spiritual realm.
Therefore, put on the whole armor of God, and let
prayer just take the helm.
Finally, fight the good fight. In God we win,
because it is a fixed fight.
Keep the oil flowing in your life, with a pure heart,
while shining bright!!

Abba God, The Master Poet
5/1/2024

Abba God, the Master poet, straight powerful.
Who would have ever, ever thought?
Every good gift and every perfect gift is from above, and it is
not for nought.

Abba God, the Master poet! His gifts are without
repentance, because He's supernaturally great!
Please embrace your own, stay in your lane,
and don't covet anything from my plate!

Abba God, the Master poet, oh it does not get any clearer
than that!
God, Supernaturally great; yesterday, today, and forever-
more! I'd trademark that on a hat!

Abba God, the Master poet, I wear Your love like a Bible
verse written on a sleeve.
All I have to do moving forward, is Obey, have Faith, Trust
and Believe!!

Abba God, The Master Poet

Abba God, the Master poet, please hide thy word in my heart as a constant reminder.
So, I can live a holy life, holding hands with Your wisdom, as my lawful, good guide.

Reflection

Who do you think each poem within the section "Abba God, The Master Poet" is written to?

What comes to mind as you read each poem in this section?

What's your favorite line (s) in each poem within this section?

If you had to add another stanza to each poem within this section, what would you write?

Other Thoughts

Acknowledgments

A kind and sincere thank you to the True and Living God, for blessing me with this dope gift to write beautiful poetry, that will encourage the lives of many, for His glory.

To my family, and those, who encouraged me throughout this book writing journey, thank you so very much!

To the blessed helpers along the way, who assisted in bringing this vision to pass, Mr. and Mrs. Moore, Cynthia Portalatin (editor), and to the supporters, past, present and future, a wonderful thank you goes out to you all!